Empath and Psychic Abilities

A Survival Guide for Highly Sensitive People. Guided Meditations to Open Your Third Eye, Expand Mind Power, Develop Telepathy, Intuition and Clairvoyance

Mindfulness Academy

Table of Contents

Introduction

Sympathy is simply the other name of pity, but an empath walks that extra mile to understand why someone is behaving the way they are behaving, and they do everything they can to alleviate other people's pain.

But empaths need to nurture their quality in order to truly be able to use it to the best of their abilities. On top of that, if you are a psychic empath, it will be even harder for you to spend your day-to-day life because you can literally feel all the energies surrounding you.

But in this book, we will learn how you can prevent yourself from getting overwhelmed by emotions and how to practice greater control over life, in general.

Chapter 1:

Who Is a Psychic Empath?

Some people are blessed to have extrasensory perception, allowing them to see, feel, or hear information that is otherwise hidden and not perceivable to the normal human senses.

These blessed people are often referred to as psychics, and in this modern era, psychics are devoted to helping other people.

What Is Psychic Power?

The word "power" can be referred to in regards to a number of aspects. For psychics, their psychic powers come from deep knowledge, learning, and understanding of their abilities.

They utilize their extrasensory perception to harness the energy around them to perform "powerful acts" that help other people. Since all of 'us' humans are intelligent beings with a soul, we surely do have innate natural "psychic" powers, sometimes referred to as our sixth sense. However, only some are more sensitive and attuned to these abilities so that they can harness these abilities into "powers" after they have studied and practiced these abilities.

However, this does not imply that psychics are able to get in tune with them as soon as they are born. If a person wants to harness and build this psychic energy, the individual must be spiritually and mentally connected to his or her inner and higher self.

To be able to connect and respond to the different forces around them that are beyond the range of ordinary human perception, one needs to go through constant learning and training. With a sense of purpose, psychics choose to develop and harness these abilities so that they are able to help other people.

Certain planetary placements in birth charts, card spreads, or even casual conversations with regards to manifestations and such can reveal an individual's psychic abilities and perceptions to another psychic practitioner such as a tarot card reader, an astrologer, an occult practitioner, and so on.

Although a lot of people might think how amazing it is to possess and be able to harness such a powerful ability, being a psychic person does not come easy, and many people have misconceptions about what this gift actually entails. Working with psychic skills requires a considerable amount of patience, self-love, and practice.

From an early age, a majority of us are warned by our elders to be cautious when it comes to the services of psychic practitioners as scams and, hence, we begin to perceive and associate psychic gifts and abilities, at large, as dubious and fraudulent.

Some of the otherwordly or psychic experiences we come across as children are also, therefore, discredited, and even if we incline towards exploring divination practices in adulthood, we are still quick to raise an eyebrow and start to doubt when we hear the word "psychic." While there are many charlatans for sure who either exaggerate their skills or make them up entirely, these kinds of people are definitely not psychics, but they are con artists who use manipulation and fear tactics to prey on gullible and vulnerable targets.

However, it is crucial to know that truly psychic people, on the other hand, are simply individuals who are able to see, hear, feel, sense, taste, or have intuition beyond the boundaries of the physical world and ordinary human beings. As individuals start to expand their sensory spectrum and continue to explore this psychic realm more, it becomes abundantly clear that some senses become increasingly less common among psychic individuals. It is through this awareness that many psychic individuals become fully aware of their unique, inherent psychic abilities and powers.

Fundamentally, psychic skills or powers are defined by an innate ability to process sensory data, both tangible and intangible stimuli, on an extremely deep emotional, physical, or spiritual level. Obviously, this is rather a very broad definition of psychic power. Extrasensory gifts vary greatly in intensity and application; it is best and easier to imagine psychic skills on a spectrum.

Here is an example of a psychic spectrum:

To visualize a psychic spectrum, imagine four friends meeting for lunch. The first individual to arrive greets the host and takes her table, notices her table is missing a fork, sees that her glass is already filled with wine, and takes a sip out of it as she is feeling thirsty and waits for her friends.

The second individual comes in, sees that the host is scrolling through his phone, and senses that he might be bored or under stress, and greets the host warmly. The host welcomes him, and he then joins his friend at the table. The third friend enters the restaurant, and as she is approaching the host, she is overwhelmed with stimuli.

She notices the restaurant's garish decor, the servers' swift movements, and a distinguishingly loud gentleman at the back who is dominating the conversation. She can feel that the energy that this particular person is radiating is arrogant and abrasive, and his company seems to be both uncomfortable and embarrassed.

She then starts to wonder how his children will grow up to be like. Will they grow up adopting this behavior from their parent, or will they reject it and become soft and docile? Suddenly the third friend is snapped back into reality as the host greets her.

Once she arrives at the table, she starts to discuss her observations with her other friends. Finally, the fourth friend arrives at the restaurant, and upon his arrival, he feels extremely overwhelmed by the lights, the sound, the movement, the smell, and the overall energy inside the place.

Within a few seconds, he becomes aware of the internal personal dynamics at each table, the complex relationships of the people there, the pungent smell of a certain dish that links back to his past memories, a few charred rafters on the ceiling. He starts to wonder if there had been a fire there recently that had caused the charred rafters. Suddenly, he senses extreme heaviness and knows that there had been something very bad in that restaurant. He becomes nervous and trying to shake off the feeling; he ignores the host and hurries over to his friends. However, this feeling persists throughout lunch even when he tries to ignore them, exhausting him.

Hence, we can see that the first two friends demonstrated a relatively standard range of sensitivity, while the latter two friends demonstrate more extreme extrasensory abilities. This is how the psychic spectrum operates as the power and the sensory abilities vary from one psychic individual to another.

What Does It Mean To Be Psychic?

The word "psychic" gets thrown around a lot and in meanings that are misunderstood and mistaken, but what does it actually mean? The word "psychic" comes from the Greek word "psykhikos" which means "of the soul." A psychic is a person who has a strong sensory perception that enables them to foresee things and connect to other energies and spirits.

Their sixth sense or intuition enables them to experience unusual things, have visions of the future, or have strong telepathy experiences.

You will be surprised to learn that you can show signs of this gift and not even realize it, and that is because the signs, although almost bizarre, still often seem relatively meaningless to us.

Here are some signs that might actually mean you are psychic:

1. ***Frequent Deja Vu Experiences*** - Although the cause of Deja Vu is widely researched and debated, and science does have a physiological reason, however, if you experience it very frequently, it is often cited as a sign that you have psychic abilities.
2. ***Sensations Around Third Eye*** - The Third Eye is the space between your eyebrows. If you feel any kind of sensation or pressure, it could be because your chakras are opening up, and you are beginning to pick up on psychic signals.

3. ***Looking At The Clock At The Same Time*** - It is known that spirits try to communicate with the living through signs, and repeating numbers are said to be such signs, for example, 1111 or 111. Numerology has a divine meaning for each number and if you happen to look at the clock at the same time very often, look up the meaning behind the number. These messages could be a sign of channeling psychic ability.

4. ***Strong and Vivid Dreams*** - Do you frequently have vivid dreams where you can even recall the most minute of details? Do you experience the same dreams? Do most of your dreams come true or have a meaning or message behind them? All of these are known to be signs of psychic abilities.

5. ***Psychometric Experiences*** - Psychometry enables you to sense the history of an object, place, or person by touching them. You would often find a psychic holding the hand of a person and experiencing his past.

What Are The Different Types Of Psychic Abilities?

Seeing into the future is a natural occurrence, and we all are psychics only varying in degree. Time is simultaneous, and there is no past or future to our eternal self, that is, our true nature. To the eternal self, there is only the eternal now; everything happens at once.

The term psychic is generally used to describe a person with the ability to recognize things that are hidden from the five basic senses and are able to sense something through the use of extrasensory perception.

Being a psychic is actually a generalized umbrella term that is used to describe different forms of psychic abilities. There are many types of psychic powers, and all of them have distinguished ways of sharing information and perceiving things.

Everyone possesses varying degrees of psychic abilities, from a simple"gut instinct" through to foreseeing future events; here are some of the most common and talked about psychic abilities:

1. ***Clairvoyance*** - Also known as "clear seeing," it is an interior vision. Clairvoyant mediums have the ability to "see" things presented to them in the mind's eye or the Third eye. They see these visions as mental flashes, including pictures as people, scenes, places, objects, spirits, symbols, and colors. Clairvoyance is seeing

beyond what the ordinary eyes see. It is also possible to receive many visual insights and see the auras of people, animals, and even plants using clairvoyance. Those with excellent clairvoyant senses are even known to see fairies, spirits, angels, and many other spiritual beings. Often a clairvoyant medium can see objects or symbols which may have a specific personal or universal meaning, as well as light anomalies such as flashing lights, orbs, and sparks. It is a psychic seeing, and it is essential to note that every clairvoyant medium has different depictions of what they see and how they see it. You can think of it as a sort of screen that pops up before them to provide information and messages in the form of pictures, symbols, and so on. It may also show up as a visual of a person with distinct characteristics or a warning of a future scenario. They may see a person with their distinct visual characteristics or warn you of a scenario they see in your future.

2. ***Clairaudience*** - Also known as "clear hearing," clairaudience is the ability to hear messages from the spirit realm. In this type of psychic ability, messages are transmitted directly into the mind of the clairaudience medium. At times the medium may hear a non-descript voice call their name or a mix of voices as if they are listening to a radio. It is the ability to hear beyond the

physical hearing of an ordinary individual. This is what is known as inner hearing. Those who are clairaudient mediums hear many different things such as bells, voices, music, and sounds. Sound is of extreme importance to the metaphysical and spiritual traditions throughout the entire world. Most of the time, before an important insight is received or as an opening to a spiritual experience occurs, a sound is heard through clairaudience. This sound may be a soft ring in the ear, a quiet whisper, or sometimes it may be much more intense. It is also known in some traditions that this sound is referred to as the bells of paradise or the trumpeting before the gates. The sounds heard through the clairaudience are often described as radio signals from varying levels of universal airwaves, including our own higher self. The voices that can be heard through clairaudience are often described as giving spiritual guidance or warning of impending danger.

3. ***Clairsentience*** - Also known as "sensing feelings," clairsentience is most commonly described as gut feeling or intuition. Clairsentient mediums have the ability to sense and feel emotions from the spiritual realm, both positive and negative. These feelings are being transmitted from their guides and are very distinctly and clearly different from the medium's own

feelings. The mediums can receive warnings or information this way as in feeling that something is not right or get an excited, elated feeling when something wonderful is about to happen. It can also be described as empathy with the ability to feel or sense information beyond the physical sense. This is a tactile psychic feeling. For instance, an example of clairsentience would be shaking hands with a person and almost instantly feeling comfort sparked by their touch as if you have known them all throughout your life. This is an example of clairsentience, also known as psychic sensory experiences. These vibrations and energies are meant to clue the medium into the particular feeling itself for gaining extraordinary information.

4. ***Clairalience*** - It is basically the sense of smell, only heightened and attuned to clairalience medium beyond the physical sense of smell. It is the ability to sense or smell a particular fragrance or odor that is being transmitted by the spirit. Each time, the other people around are not able to usually sense or smell the odor. It can be related to the spirit who is sending the message, such as smelling cigarettes or pipe tobacco for someone who smoked or the person's favorite perfume or fragrance.

5. ***Clairgustance*** - This type of psychic ability is linked to the sense of taste. The medium has the ability to taste the essences being transmitted b the spirit. A spirit can transfer a character or behavior influence to the mediums, and sometimes it comes to them in the form of a flavor. This is usually something that they really loved and enjoyed while they were in the body.

6. ***Clairtangency*** - Also known as psychometry, the mediums with this type of psychic ability are able to receive a message by touching or holding an object in their hands. The object is usually personal and contains the vibration and energy of the owner in the composition or the material of the item. By doing this, they can tell the personality of the owner and perhaps see, hear, or feel situations that are going on around the person, past or present. Psychometry is the ability or art of deriving information about people or events associated with an object solely by touching or being near it. Objects belonging to a person are used to help induce psychic intuitions about them. This ability to touch an object, item, or person and receive information about them can be received in mind as pictures, a moving short film, or a sudden knowing of information.

7. ***Remote Viewing*** - Remote viewing is a form of clairvoyance and is known as the process of observing

from a great distance. This psychic ability allows the remote viewer to see what is happening in another place describing details about the target that is inaccessible to the normal senses.

Psychics usually have one or more of these gifts, which can be used on their own or all together. Among these, the most commonly found ability among psychics is clairsentience. Having one to three psychic abilities in one person is usually common; however, having all the abilities is very rare.

Popular Myths Surrounding Psychics

1. ***Psychic Mediums are Scammers*** - One of the most popular myths that surround the whole concept of psychic abilities and mediums is that they scam people and use cold reading to con men and women. In almost every industry, it is usually common to find fraudulent people who treat others unfairly and take advantage of them; hence, similarly, these types of people are also present in the psychic industry as any other industry. However, in this industry, con artists are generally pretty easy to spot.

   They make claims of having the ability to help you and make you money or save you from bad luck and bad finances. These scammers are usually not around for very long as they always end up with a bad reputation earned by their dubious and fraudulent activities and claims.

Most true psychics are genuinely gifted, though in varying degrees, at what they do and will generally have the client's best interest in their mind. The psychic industry is greatly unpoliced, and if a person is clever and bold enough to engage in scams, they are able to trick those that are vulnerable. However, it is important to keep in mind that when choosing a psychic or a medium, always do your research and ask others for feedback and recommendations.

2. ***If Psychic People Were Real, It Would Be Easier to Find Missing People*** - Although these types of cases are scarce and do not happen very often, there have been several real-life cases wherein psychics or mediums have helped to solve murder cases. It is not as simple as it sounds to get involved in a murder or a missing person's case as a psychic or a medium.

   The medium may be able to connect with the spirit of the person in question, and they can be provided with various information such as impressions of the circumstances surrounding their deaths, including locations. However, there may often be dozens or even hundreds of different sites that may match the impressions that the medium was provided with. Much of the information that is received with regards to murder cases is usually very general and not specific enough to be of any real help in finding their bodies.

Even when psychics do have a piece of specific information, it can be very difficult to find a connection that will lead to a breakthrough in the case. Although, with the right circumstances and a good connection, psychics can be of valuable importance in the cases of finding missing persons, however, unfortunately, there are just too many factors that affect the information and how the mediums relate to it. Therefore, it is often not precise enough.

3. ***Psychics Can Read Minds*** - Psychics and mediums cannot and do not read other people's minds. They are definitely able to tune into your individual energy field that contains information about your life; however, they cannot just simply read your mind or know what you are thinking at any given time.

   Mediums and psychics receive information through their psychic senses about the person they are connecting with, and information comes through to them in bits and pieces. They may see images, hear brief sounds and noises, voices or words, get a glimpse of a particular smell or taste, and/or feel an energy shift in different parts of their bodies, indicating a message or information. This information can be about places, events, or people related to their past, present, or future.

4. ***Psychics Research Their Audience*** - another one of the most common myths that people believe is that psychics or mediums research everyone present in their audience before a show.

   However, this is very rare and even very difficult for a person to do so. Perhaps with some expertise and time, it would be possible to gather some background information on some people attending the show; however, that person is required to study the information and memorize it.

   The amount of time and effort required to do so is not simply worth it. It is much easier and logical for a psychic to tune into their abilities than it would be to do all that research and memorizing before each show.

5. ***Psychics Predict Future*** - Psychic and mediums do not actually predict the future.

   However, what they can do is that they tune into energies connected to the future events in people's lives using their psychic abilities to give insights into possible outcomes. Using tools such as tarot cards, palmistry, and astrology combined with information gathered with the help of psychic senses can often give insights into possible future events with some degree of accuracy. However, psychics are human, too, so they may misinterpret the meaning of the information they receive and can get wrong.

All of the above myths were debunked by Suzie Price, a renowned psychic who was awarded the "People's Choice Award" by the International Psychic Association in 2014.

What You Should Know About A Psychic Empath

While it is well known by now that everyone has some degree of psychic ability, it can take a number of different forms. For some people, psychic ability manifests itself as the ability to be what is known as an empath.

Empathy is the ability to sense and feel what others are feeling without their telling us verbally.

Someone who is a psychic empath often needs to learn basic shielding techniques; otherwise, they can find themselves feeling drained and exhausted after absorbing the energies of others.

The psychic form of empathy should not be confused with the basic human form of empathy, and the basic difference is that the former can pick up non-visual, non-verbal cues that another individual is feeling pain, fear, or joy.

Chapter 2: How to Enhance Your Psychic Abilities?

Psychics, as some would already know and some would be surprised to believe, are simple everyday individuals like any one of us who, along with possessing regular abilities like all of us, have the added benefit of being able to see, hear, sense, taste, feel things in more details than us.

They also have a very strong intuitive force to see beyond the boundaries of the physical world. What is the matter of concern is that it needs to be analyzed what knowledge and perceptions can be recognized as "normal" or regular by the world that we live in.

The society that we live in will otherwise have us believe that everything is either black or white. Most of the time, the nuances of things get lost in understanding as the different shades of things fail to register to the common eye. But, it is through these very regular experiences that some of us might realize how the events or the sense perceptions that we are experiencing are very different from what others are experiencing. Along with that, certain things are only becoming known to us while others are remaining oblivious to them.

These realizations make us aware that we might have some unique traits in us that others don't have and how this awareness of ours is helping us tap into our inner psychic abilities.

Psychic abilities in a person can be described as their inherent skills or ability to process the data that are sensory, both in their tangible and intangible form, and that is to say, to understand and analyze everything in a much more deep-rooted manner.

It is where a person's emotional, physical, and spiritual plane gets heightened and much more receptive than what other people experience. But telling only this doesn't do it justice completely because the psychic spectrum is huge. So, all the other possibilities need to be kept in mind while talking about psychic abilities.

There are many ways in which a person can understand and thereby enhance their psychic abilities. Psychic abilities can emerge most of the time during a person's childhood, in cases when such abilities are passed on to the particular individual from someone else in the family who has had a great impact on the child directly or indirectly. It might also be that a person develops these psychic abilities through the environmental influence around them.

While we are growing up, however, it is common for people to hear it from the elders to stop being so sensitive to everything and to see things for what they are. That things are not always such as we find them to be, and we should take things only for their face value.

But the inherent psychic in the concerned person can't really be ignored like that. It is not so simple. The psychic abilities cannot get lost just because someone chooses to or is forced to ignore them for long.

With some work, these abilities will get polished and will be reignited. So, let us look at us how one can enhance these abilities.

Meditation

For any person to enhance their psychic abilities, it is very important to have a calm mind and a relaxed body to tap into the inner psychic in someone. One of the very first and extremely essential requirements for a practicing psychic is to be in an environment that is not disturbing to the inner soul and outer body.

An environment that is soothing to the mind so that there remain no distractions to derail the person's thoughts and concentration. For that, it is essential to practice meditation on a regular basis. It has to be made into a habit where a significant amount of time will be given behind meditating every day so that the inner core can be reached and its power can be tapped.

This is important for any person who wants to enhance their psychic abilities to reach their core with a minimum effort. It is important to connect with one's soul to understand what's going on there and help you connect with the world and the universe.

It is essential to settle on a focus point and keep your concentration fix on it. Try using a candle and fix your eyes on the flame, for example. Try and stop other thoughts from clouding your inner vision. The next thing you need to do is calm your breathing and take regular, deep, and calm breaths so that your body is in a state of rest.

You can also start with meditating while keeping your eyes open at the beginning before you get into the habit completely, by looking at trees or clouds floating by, for example. It is entirely on you to find out for yourself what works for you. As you slowly start getting into the habit of meditating, you can shift your procedure of close eye meditating.

The more focus you have, the more you can actively and successfully unravel your feelings and look beyond the apparent. Meditating will help you become more aware of your surroundings.

The next time you start getting intuitive, all your senses will become alert without misleading you or without you getting distracted. You will start getting familiar with your feelings and intuition.

Start taking Psychic Classes

Having psychic abilities only is not enough. Like every other trait or talent that a person might have, psychic abilities too need to be practiced, polished, and perfected over time. It takes a lot of diligence, determination, and patience to perfect anything and psychic abilities are no better. They need to be practiced regularly, and they need a professional training.

Otherwise, it will only be on a surface level. Only with professional training will you get to know what and how you should do things so that you can use your talents to their full extent. Psychic classes come in the picture then. With regular and proper classes on how to train yourself to enhance your psychic abilities to the fullest, you will be able to take it at your own comfort and preferred pace. You can start practicing at home even to see how things are working for you.

Nowadays, there is also no dearth of online classes that will help you get in touch with professionals who will train you to enhance your psychic abilities. These online classes cover a range of different subjects and topics that are sure to satisfy your curiosity.

That will help you find out what suits you and what you find yourself most interested in and then go on to study those subjects in further detail. Taking such classes will help you clear your doubts and come to terms with everything that you are going through. It will give you knowledge regarding things that you might otherwise have a problem talking to with others.

It will give you clarity regarding how you want to deal with things and help you get a clear picture of how things should proceed. So, if you really want to tap into your inner spirit and enhance your psychic abilities, taking classes can be really helpful for you. Instead of fumbling in the dark regarding things you are not sure of, try and get help from professionals for better results.

Take Care of Yourself and Your Body

No matter what you do, what new ventures you take, you have to keep in mind that nothing will work out if you are not healthy, both physically and mentally.

You have to take care of yourself and look after all your needs to see how much you can take, what works for you and what doesn't, what makes you happy and, what doesn't. Remember that only if you feel good from the outside and inside will anything that you do bring you success and will be enjoyable as a journey.

The same goes for when you want to channelize your inner power and enhance your psychic abilities. Remember that enhancing your psychic abilities is as much psychological labor as a physical one.

If you are doing it right, it will take you a ton of emotional and physical labor to actually bring all your core strength to their optimum power.

And as a result, it is the most natural to overlook your own needs as your mind will tend to be always preoccupied with something or other. That is the reason, no matter what you are doing, you need to keep your health in mind that realize that you are as good as your health. Take care of yourself and what your body needs.

Eat correct food at the correct time. Do regular exercises, do things that you enjoy so that you are refreshed and relaxed. Don't ignore your medical conditions if you have any. Don't go out of your way to force yourself into doing things that you don't enjoy or which is uncomfortable for you. The better your physical and emotional ability is, the easier it will be for you to enhance your psychic abilities.

Get rid of all the bad habits that you might be having, like smoking or drinking. Alcohol and tobacco are extremely bad for not only your health, but they cloud your judgment and distract you all the time. You need to have a balanced lifestyle with a proper sleep schedule for you to be at your best so as to concentrate fully on your inner abilities.

You cannot expect to give your psychic practice your best shot unless you know that you are completely ready physically and emotionally. If you are well-rested, well-fed, relaxed, and in good health, then automatically, things you do will be much more productive and successful. You will have a much better chance of enhancing your psychic abilities that way.

Work With Your Spirit Guides

Each and every one of us has spirit guides who are always there present around us to help us. They are present to assist us in all of our needs. Be it with our choices or be it with our experiences. Our guides are ever-present to look out for us and to see that everything is alright. What we need to understand that they are just a thought away. It is completely on us to realize that and feel their presence.

Whether we want to be aware of their presence or not is completely on us to decide, but their presence is something that we cannot ignore. What is essential then is to learn and know of ways in which we can connect with our Guides. We need to be aware of all such ways we can connect with them in a more conscious way so that they can help us by providing us with a more powerful and more effective tool to develop our inner abilitics.

Getting connected with our spirit guides will help us break away from the barriers of distraction and come in control of our abilities completely. We just need to be more consistent and patient in all our efforts so that we can work with our guides more because the more we work with them, the easier the connection with them will become. The easier it will be to have communication with our guides, and that will ease all our work. It is up to us how much of such a connection we allow.

The more such connections take place, the easier it will be to start believing your instincts and inner voice. The easier it will be to form insight and also trust yourself. With trust in yourself will come more confidence and self-belief. That will be like a guiding force to enhance the inner psychic in us. All we need to remember is that our guides are always present. You need to ask for their help. They will definitely work with you.

Build Trust

Always remember that a person's psychic abilities are bound to get increased and get enhanced if the person concerned trusts themselves and their intuition.

Accepting one's thoughts and emotions for what they are and by not ignoring or neglecting one's gut feelings, one's psychic abilities are sure to get stronger, and that's what any practitioner should do. You need to strongly accept and rust what you are feeling, and you need to proclaim them boldly. This is not achieved in a single day. If you feel that you indeed have psychic abilities, you need to act upon them. You need to trust your instincts, and day after day, you need to build a strong communicable bridge that will help you communicate with yourself and come to terms with all that you are feeling will become much easier.

Always keep in mind that accepting your reality and trusting what you are feeling, that is, the information you have in you, is probably the most crucial and primary thing that anyone needs to do when starting out in this path of psychic practice. In order for your practice to become perfect and in order for you to attain the utmost level of efficiency and accuracy in your practice, you need to trust yourself. The more trust you have in yourself and your abilities, the easier it will be for you to practice with efficiency. Trusting becomes a huge source of enhancing your powers and giving yourself credit for who you actually are.

Some people who have psychic abilities and yet they don't trust themselves enough with it tend to have a lot of problem with themselves because if someone has psychic abilities, it is only natural for them to feel things in a deeper way or get intuitive knowledge about something that other people will not have. Now imagine the situation where among a group of people, you are the only one who has a different feeling or a different opinion or, for that matter, different knowledge about something. If you don't trust yourself enough, you will start getting the feeling that something is wrong with you or you are acting weirdly, which you are not. Only if you trust yourself enough will you understand what the actual scenario is.

Open Your Seven Chakra Centers

Suppose you are someone who takes their psychic abilities seriously. In that case, you need to think of a stable future where you can put your abilities to use, and that only be done if you are successful in developing a strong understanding of your spiritual core. That will help you get closure with your divine attributes and will help you further your practice. One way you can do this is to open up all the seven chakra centers in your body.

If you can successfully tap into all the seven chakra centers' power, it will become all the easier to enhance your psychic abilities. Now, what are these chakra centers? So, basically, there are centers in your body, seven to be precise, where all your inner energies are focused.

By getting in touch with these centers, all the energy that exists in your body will be yours to control and command. These are the places in your body that have the most reception of psychic intuition, and if you are in contact with these chakras inside you, your psychic abilities are bound to get enhanced.

There are many ways in which a person can receive psychic information, and opening up these chakras does exactly that. It eases up the process of receiving information and channeling the power of the inner core.

It does take some practice while tapping into your chakras, but once you get them opened, things are going to be much more fluent. If you activate your chakras, your senses will be much more alert, and you will constantly be able to communicate with yourself and the outside universe.

When all the seven chakras of your body are active and working, it will also help you open your third eye, which is what helps you see things that others can't. That is what makes you a psychic.

The feeling that you get which makes you look at things differently is the power of your third eye. That power will get enhanced if you activate your chakra centers.

Practice Seeing Auras

Suppose you are someone who not only wants to enhance your psychic abilities, but you also want to do it specifically for the purpose of being in the healing profession, where you want to help others treat their medical conditions through your psychic abilities.

In that case, you need to start practicing seeing your auras. Let me explain it in detail. An aura is basically like a very vibrant ray of color that is composed of a lot of energy and flows around a person or living things in general.

It indicates the different moods that a living being possess, and our aura gives other people the first impression about us. Any person who is even a bit observant should be able to guess what kind of a personality we have given the attitude with which we start talking, and that gives away our aura.

What needs to be understood here is that there are many psychic abilities that you need to be born with in order for you to practice and develop upon them. But unlike those abilities, seeing auras is not something that you need to be born with.

This is a psychic ability that you can develop over time and keep practicing it in order to perfect it. All it takes is for you to have patience and dedication.

Some people get it easily, and after few days of practicing the art of seeing auras, they start seeing the different colors. While at the same time, others might take a bit longer to master the art of seeing the colors. The best way to see the auras or the different colors is to keep your chakra centers clean and open.

The more you tap into your chakra centers and keep them activated, the more you keep them polished, the easier it will be for you to see the auras and sense the colors. That is the reason, the more accurate you are in understanding the aura that the other person is giving out, the easier it will be for you to deal with that person and tackle the situations that might arise.

Use Psychometry

To understand what psychometry is, it is basically the power that a person with psychic abilities possess where they can understand traits about a certain person or get useful information about that person by touching the possessions of that person.

As a psychic, this is a very useful power to have, and in order to enhance their psychic abilities more, this power of psychometry needs to be practiced. With more practice, a person can tone this power into a powerful source of extracting information about others. After a point, he\she will be able to extend this to strangers as well, were given something in their possessions, getting to know things about them will become an easy task.

However, when a person is just starting out, it is better to start off with the possessions of someone whom they are really close with so that understanding things becomes easier. The closer that person is to you, the more familiar you are with that person's belongings, the easier it will be for you to understand and get more information. Practicing psychometry is one of the most prominent ways of enhancing your psychic abilities.

As a practitioner, you need to sense any impression that you might feel of that concerned person whose objects you have taken. This will develop a kind of bridge between you and that concerned person, and this mode of communication is bound to strengthen your psychic powers. Unlike some other practices, psychometry is one that you as a practitioner can start working on very soon and can start developing upon from the very beginning. As a practitioner, you will be surprised to see how fast and how smoothly you can develop this skill as it usually comes very fast to people who have psychic powers.

Take Help of Other Useful Tools

Along with all the above-mentioned ways in which you can enhance your psychic abilities, there are some tools that can come in really handy while practicing psychic abilities. Tools such as tarot cards, for example, or pendulum are very easy to learn and very useful at the same time.

All you need to do is learn about these tools in detail as to how they should be used, what angle they should be kept at, which hand you should keep them, and what your body language must be like while you are using them. Remember that these tools are basically the agents that will help you get in touch with your inner core of power and your higher self. They will help you get the necessary information that you need in your psychic practice, helping you get answers to questions that you had been seeking out.

Maintain a Journal

Let us understand this now that no matter what powers you might have, they won't ever add up to much unless you want them to.

Your powers are as good as you are. They will be as strong as you want them to by working hard. So, if at all you are serious about enhancing and developing your psychic abilities, you will need to make many conscious decisions about them.

You will need to keep track of all that you want to achieve through these powers, all the new things you want to learn, and all the new things you have to practice. It is not always possible to keep everything in mind, and things might get lost in the process. That is why you need to maintain a proper journal where you need to put in all the necessary things for your practice.

Try writing down all the questions that you might be having at any given point so that you can go back to them when in need and you can find answers to them. You need to be diligent and systematic about the entire process so that no stone remains unturned and so that you might not regret it later.

The key is to pay attention to proper attention to all your dreams and keep them right in front of you to constantly remind you of what they are and what you need to do about them.

Psychic abilities are certain powers that many people are gifted with. They are gifts of nature, and they can be enabled within a person by tapping into their chakra centers. Psychic abilities help a person see beyond what is the normal realm of existence that we are accustomed to.

People with psychic abilities have the power to sense and see what others can't, and every person possesses some of these powers to a lesser or higher degree.

What matters is then to tap into them, and if a person is interested enough, then to practice them and perfect them eventually.

All the points mentioned above will be helpful in enhancing the psychic abilities of a person, and if someone decides to pursue their powers seriously, these ways are sure to be helpful in their way.

Psychic abilities are unique gifts of communication that a person is endowed with, and they should be wasted. Trusting oneself and diligently keep at practicing them is the key that can help a person polish their skills and excel in their practice.

Keeping alert and activating one's chakra centers will definitely help a person understand everything that is going on, making the entire process easier for them.

Chapter 3: Communicating With Your Spirit Guides

Spirit guides are entities that are not human but which act as a protector, a guide, or an advisor for human beings. These entities have a strong rooting in different thought schools of Western spiritualism, and spirit guides have now become a much more commonly discussed topic in everyday lives, and people are gradually opening up to the idea of actively seeking out support from their spirit guides. This chapter is the perfect read for you if you are trying to learn more about this topic, as it will take you through the basics about the different kinds of spirit guides and the ways in which you can establish a connection with them and then strengthen it further.

Types of Spirit Guides

Spirit guides vary in what they stand for and how they are related to you. This means that some spirit guides have been with you for the entire duration of your life, while on the other hand, certain spirit guides have been with you from even before you were born, and certain other kinds only enter your life as and when you need their presence. Therefore, there can be different kinds of spirit guides, and each of them serves a different purpose in our lives, which is why there are also various ways to connect with each of them. Six different kinds of common spirit guides have been described below:

1. **Guardian Angels:** Perhaps the most commonly known spirit guides, guardian angels belong to you completely and exclusively (unlike other spirit guides who can at once cater to the needs of multiple people). Your guardian angel has devoted their entire life to helping you out solely, which means that you can turn to them at any moment for immediate and urgent

assistance. These angels help people from all religions, spiritual faiths, and beliefs, making them non-denominational in nature. Finally, unlike some other kinds of spirit guides, your guardian angel will love you unconditionally and forever

2. **Archangels:** Archangels are considered to be the leaders in the world of angels, and they usually possess a considerably large energy signature. When you invite an archangel into your life, you would- in all likelihood-feel a shift in the overall energy levels in the room. This is especially bound to happen if you are very sensitive to energy or are an empath. Different archangels come with their own distinct specialties; for example, the Archangel Raphael is best known for working on healing and can work with almost countless people at once, unlike other Archangels who have a limited pool of energy.

3. **Departed Loved Ones:** As their name suggests, these spirit guides are deceased family members or other loved ones who choose to actively extend your support even after them having passed away, and their help is extended in the most real and practical ways- since they were once very much a part of your everyday life- which might include nurturing a certain troubled relationship which you are a part of or sending suitable job

opportunities your way. However, your spirit guide does not necessarily have to be a person with whom you were very close during their lifespan. Even loved ones whom you did not know very well personally but were attached to in any form can be very helpful spirit guides. This also extends to the idea that any human who was once living and with whom you can identify some sort of common ground can become your spirit guide. For example, suppose you are a singer. In that case, the chances are that you can have a spirit guide by your side which was once a singer or performer and now just wants to help you with figuring out the artistic aspects of your life, and this can happen despite you not having known the person very well.

4. **Spirit Animals:** Your spirit animal is most likely to be a pet from your past who was really close to you and had passed away, after which they have become a part of your larger squad of spiritual guidance. Besides that, spirit animals could also be an animal which has the potential to teach you something. An example of this would be how wolves can teach you the significance of meeting your survival needs on your own or how a peacock has the capability to make you realize how to confidently own your own qualities. You can meet your spirit animal for the first time in many ways- you could

chance upon them in a dream, randomly through some merchandise, or even in your backyard.

5. **Helper Angels:** These angels are the spirit guides which perhaps have the least personal attachment to you. They act as 'freelance' spirit guides, which implies that they are simply looking for humans to connect with and help out in specific situations during which they seek some kind of support and guidance.

   This help can range anywhere from finding a suitable office space to finding friends during a difficult phase in their lives.

6. **Ascended Masters:** Ascended masters refer to spirit guides who were actually once human beings and lived their personal journeys of great spiritual development and influence. Some examples of this would include deceased personalities such as Mother Mary or Buddha, both of whom- among many others- were humans at one point in time but are now occupying a special place in the world of spirits and can act as spiritual teachers or guides to human beings. A common idea about ascended masters is that all of them are actually partners, and they work together regardless of the religion, faith, or culture they belonged to when they were alive and were on the earth.

Effective Ways to Communicate with Spirit Guides

Our spirit guides often communicate with us by sending different signs our way. These signs are also known as synchronicities- which has been defined by the famous psychiatrist Carl Jung as "a meaningful coincidence."

An example of this would be that perhaps you need to improve the relationship you share with your parents and that is something which has been on your mind for some time, and out of the blue, you notice a book on your friend's shelf the very next day which addresses communication issues between parents and their children. This can very well be a 'meaningful coincidence' that has been sent your way by your spirit guide, who has been aware of the issues which have been bothering you and wants to give you a nod in the right direction.

Spirit guides can also communicate with you by using number sequences, musical messages, or even dreams. You might come across a possible solution to a problem that you have been tackling with, in your dream, and work on that to fix your real-life problem, or you might find out that the song that you find inspiring or uplifting just happens to be playing on the radio after you have had a long, tiring day. Another way in which they communicate with you is by sending helpful opportunities and people your way.

This is when you chance upon an opportunity which will only work out if you actively act upon it, and not otherwise, but the way in which you find it can be absolutely random and unprecedented (examples of this could be impulsively purchasing a ticket to a workshop which goes on to change your life, or asking an intriguing new person out for lunch, and so on).

These are ways in which your spirit guide is communicating with you, not just about the problems you are facing but also letting you know that they are aware of your hardships and are willing to lend a helping hand when you need one.

Listed below are 12 effective ways which could help you communicate with your spirit guides –

Try to be present in your daily life

Often, when you are too busy and caught up with your daily lives, it becomes hard for you to be mindful of everything else that is taking place around you.

This also makes it difficult for you to rightly spot the spiritual wisdom and guidance that your guides send your way regularly. Therefore, the first step to communicate with your spirit guides would include you to be more aware and live in the moment so that you can recognize the messages they have already been sending.

Example: You can try making some open space in your daily schedule, or you can remove some responsibilities from your routine if that is feasible for you. Doing this will make sure that you would not be running around as much as you usually do, and you can use that time up to be more present in your surroundings and notice small messages from your spirit guides.

You can also use the time to get into the practice of meditation and other relaxation techniques, which might help you clear your mind out and make more space to welcome the help that is trying to find you.

Build yourself a sacred space

Another thing you can do- which goes hand-in-hand with the previous prompt- is to create a quiet, sacred space for yourself that will help you connect with your inner spirituality, in turn helping you communicate better with your spirit guides.

The realm of the earth is pretty heavy, and it is not the most comfortable place for spirits to exist in, which is why making this space would not benefit just you but your guides as well, at the same time.

In this sacred space, you can try and raise the intensity of your own spiritual energy, which will actually help your spirit guides meet you halfway on your journey of spiritual development and guidance.

Maintain a special spirit guide journal

Journaling is always a good solution to keep track of important things in your life, and if you are just beginning to connect with your spirit guides, maintaining a special journal specifically dedicated to this can be really helpful. This journal can be a safe space for you to write down the signs that you are receiving from your guides, and putting all of them in one place over a period of time can also help you identify patterns and trends among these signs. Besides doing this, you can also use your journal to write down your requests for help and guidance from your guides and let them assess your needs.

Example: To kickstart your spirit guides journal, write a letter to your guides at the start of the next week to express how grateful you feel for all the help you have received from them for navigating the tough situations in your life.

This will also get you into the habit of communicating with your guides through writing, which is a practice you will need to be closely in touch with once you start updating your journal.

After you write this letter down, also note down very briefly the areas for which you seek assistance from your guides during the week. Spend the week jotting down any synchronicities you might notice specifically pertaining to those areas.

Keep an eye out for signs from your spirit guides

You will slowly start to recognize more signs sent by your spirit guides as you increase the time and effort you put into looking for these signs. However, while being open-minded and receptive, also make sure that you are not forcing anything upon yourself in the process and are not mistaking occurrences that are not signs of being otherwise.

Also, the more you start picking up on the signs, your spirit guides will understand that you are becoming more mindful and aware about the channels of communication between the both of you, and they would then be more likely to send even more signs along your way.

Example: Remind yourself about how your guide is sending you messages while you are in the middle of daily, mundane tasks- such as washing your hair or catching the bus to work. Especially if you are going through a hard and indecisive time in your life, you can expect the situation to be navigated by the signs and guidance which are being sent to you by your spirit guides.

Get to identify and know your spirit guides

It might help the process of communication if you become more accustomed to your guides in a way in which they start feeling close and more familiar with you.

One of the first and most useful steps of establishing this connection is by giving your spirit guide a name that you can use to identify them easily.

The name you select for them can be anything you feel comfortable with- it can be a name which you have always felt a certain fondness for, or it can also be the name of a character from your favorite novel, and so on.

Giving your spirit guide a name is important because, in a way, this makes them appear more real, which will also motivate you to try and communicate with them regularly.

Once you start communicating more closely and more frequently with them, you might even be able to learn more about their personalities and the ways in which they function over time.

Example: Try to find a name for any one of your spirit guides. You can do this through simply your intuition or through using particular synchronicity, or else, you can also just be creative and come up with a name you feel some positive attachment towards.

Allow your spirit guides to join you

Many spirit guides will not interfere with you if you are not personally welcoming them into your lives. You can practice this exercise to put into place an invitation which would make your guides feel more welcome and will help them reach out to you better –

a) Relax and try to clear your mind. You can do that by meditating or by taking some deep breaths. Next, try to create a clear space in your mind into which you will invite your guide to enter.

b) You can call out to your guide and let them know that you have created a safe space for them to enter. Once you have done that, you need to check for any signs which might indicate that your guide is now present with you.

   You do not have to force anything. Just try to be as open-minded about possibilities as you could be at that moment and let things happen to you organically.

c) Try to merge all your energies into one channel, and when you feel ready, you can call out to your guide and let them know that you are ready for their assistance and support. You can also try to let them know what is wrong in your life at the moment and what sort of help might help you take care of those situations.

d) As you sit there, in your sacred space, with your guide, trying to sense the thoughts that are being projected into your mind, let yourself be free of all inhibitions and allow your guide to let you know of any thoughts or feelings they want to you transmit.

e) Once you feel that you cannot continue this and the time has come when you need to stop the session, thank your guide and let them know their support has been well-received on your part.

   Take some deep, relaxing breaths to center yourself back into your body. Next, become aware of your body- starting with your toes, and go all the way upwards to your head. Inhale and exhale while being mindful of the recent spiritual exchange and the ways in which it can change your life.

Work on improving your intuition

Helping build a better sense of intuition can help you communicate with your spirit guides better, as it will also make sure that you are being more receptive to the signs they are sending out for you.

Intuition is something we all have, and we all can also improve it through study and regular practice. There are four major types of intuitive pathways that you can try and develop further.

These paths include (a) clairaudience, or hearing voices, (b) clairvoyance, or seeing visuals, (c) clairsentience, or identifying feelings, and (d) claircognizance, or knowing things. By sharpening these four 'clair'-s, you can be in better touch with your guides.

You can also try and figure out which of the four intuitive feelings you are the strongest at and then work towards sharpening that specifically instead of trying to build all four of them up, as being considerably strong in any of them would naturally give you a headstart into things.

Example: You can practice your intuition to make smaller decisions in your life that would not impact you negatively in the larger scheme of things. Such decisions can include picking a place for lunch or choosing an outfit for a casual day.

By starting with smaller, more trivial decisions, you are already actively working on improving your intuition skills so that, in time, they can be utilized to make greater decisions in your life.

Send your guides a message through your thoughts

This might sound like the quickest and the easiest way to connect with your spirit guides, and it might look very simplistic, but more often than not- this actually works.

There are multiple ways of doing this.

You can send your guides a more formal prayer to seek their blessings; on the other hand, you can also simply communicate your needs and your gratitude towards them in merely a couple of sentences in your thoughts.

This tip can be especially useful for times when you perhaps do not havc your spirit guide's journal handy or need a quick breather in between a hectic day.

Example: Once you are done with reading this chapter, communicate your thoughts with your guides and inform them about one thing which you have been worried about over the past few days.

However, do not leave it only up to them to fix; try and talk to a friend or a loved one about it as well, and you would soon receive the help that you need- through advice, synchronicities, or maybe both of those at once.

Explore different tools for divination

There are numerous divination tools that have helped humans establish contact with the world of spirits for centuries now.

To better communicate with your guides, you can turn to one (or more) of such tools as well. Some of the most commonly accessible divination tools include tarot cards, oracle cards, runes, etc.

You can check out and indulge in various of these methods to figure out which one works the best for you and then divert your focus to that exclusively.

Example: Before getting to work with your tool of choice, hold your cards (or other similar items) in your hand and close your eyes for a minute. Then, take a few deep breaths, center yourself, and then move on to asking your spirit guides to send you a healing message through this method of divination.

Surrender something over to your guides

When you feel stuck, helpless, or frustrated about a particular situation or get the feeling that you are losing control, you can attempt to surrender the concern completely over to your spirit guides.

This might help you out in different ways, but most importantly, it will at least be effective in giving yourself a break, which will help you regain composure. You can utilize this break to explore fresh, new insights about things.

At the same time, your guides would also enjoy more freedom to do their thing to help you out without your interference of any sort in the process.

Example: Even if only temporarily, practice energetically venting out an issue to your spirit guide. Do this, and simultaneously let your mind enjoy some quiet instead of constantly being engaged in strategizing.

To do this, you can also use affirmations such as *I am handing this issue over to my guides because I trust their sense of guidance.*

Develop short and long term spiritual practices

Building and nurturing certain spiritual practices will help you be more in sync with your spiritual side, which will help facilitate better communication with your guides.

Spiritual practices can be daily, weekly, or even monthly.

Some of these can include drawing one oracle card every morning to get some inspiration, signing up for a yoga class that takes place every week, or turning up for monthly spiritual gatherings.

These activities will help you develop a deeper level of intimacy with your spirit guides, besides aiding the journey of you discovering your spirituality.

Example: You can start with trying to develop a new practice in the coming weeks, such as a new moon or a full moon ritual, which will help you create the mindset of building regular spiritual practices in your life.

Other than that, you can also try listing down the different spiritual beliefs which act as important guiding principles for you. These will also help you understand your spiritual side better.

Make efforts to learn more about spirit guides

Last but not least, being more involved in how spirituality manifests and functions can help you form a better chain of communication with your guides.

Researching on spirit guides in your leisure time is bound to strengthen the connection that you are trying to build with them.

You can also reach out to experts on this matter to know more and read or gain more information on spirit guides that empower and heal, as that would further reinforce the faith you place in your guides.

You can gain knowledge by reading and through more interactive methods such as attending an online course or a workshop on this, or even by just striking up a conversation with like-minded people.

Chapter 4: Gemstones for Psychic Abilities

Psychic abilities can be greatly enhanced by the use of different kinds of gemstones as they help a person get in touch with their inner spirit and tap into the core of power and energy that resides in them.

Gemstones can be of great help as they help a person to open their third eye and see into their inner walls of wisdom, and these stones can increase a person's intuition which is a must for a person who is practicing psychic powers. The powers of the person are sure to get stronger if the correct stones are put to use.

There are a host of various gemstones that are used for different purposes, and proper knowledge about them is a must. This chapter shall deal with some basic gemstones that are useful to a psychic.

What are Gemstones?

A piece of rock or mineral will be called a gemstone when it has been cut with precision and polished properly, and it has been used as a piece to enhance and decorate a piece of jewelry or has been used as a form of any other accessory.

Gemstones are usually made from minerals, but they could also be made from other materials like lapis lazuli or, say, amber. It depends on their hardness, which can be measured in the Moh scale of hardness as to what extent they can be used. If they are not hard enough, they will be brittle and won't be able to be used in jewelry.

If one is to know in detail about a particular gemstone and examine its quality, then the four Cs need to be thoroughly examined, and they are Colour, Clarity, Cut, and Carat. Buying a gemstone is not easy as people can be easily duped into believing it is of good quality when it is not. So, a thorough prior knowledge is important.

Best Gemstones for Enhancing Psychic Abilities

Psychic abilities can be greatly enhanced by the use of different gemstones as they each have a unique quality about themselves.

Whatever "hunches" one might get or "visions" one might see through their individual psychic abilities can be enhanced through gemstones. That is why gemstones are very popular among psychic and shamas and turret readers. Let us see a few of these gemstones and their uses.

Alexandrite

This stone falls under the family of chrysoberyl family of stones and is a very rare stone indeed. On the Moh's scale, it sits at 8.5, which basically means it is one of the hardest stones on earth. Don't mistake them for being a member of the emerald or morganite family, though.

This stone is well sought after because it helps bring happiness in a person's life, and not only that, it helps a person tap into their inner strengths and find for themselves their own source of happiness without having to depend on anyone.

What it also does is to facilitate the awareness of beauty in others and oneself, which invariably helps a person become happier than what they were used to being. After using this stone, a person is bound to become more appreciative of things that they have, thereby giving them more reasons to celebrate life.

Alexandrite provides a person with hope by helping the concerned person to become more aware of everything that is happening around them and helps them identify more possibilities around them, and as a result of this, naturally, a person can make use of things around them and grab more opportunities to become happy.

This gemstone is usually marked as the birthstone for those who are born in the month of June but then again, as they are really rare, it becomes a task getting hold of them. They are costly so if your jeweler offers them at a lower price, make sure you find out whether it is real or not.

Amethyst

This is one of the most popular gemstones of all time, be it for using them in jewelry or for enhancing psychic abilities. They are actively used for crystal healing.

There are usually two kinds of amethyst, black amethyst, which means that it has an inclusion of hematite, and thus it appears to be deep dark in color mixed with the original deep purple.

And the other is Moroccan amethyst which is deep purple in color, and it usually contains chevrons and a crackle-look to it and also violet fire. It has a seven on the Moh scale of hardness.

This stone has a lot of benefits and thus is so popular. It tends to start vibrating with a high frequency while at the same time creating a bubble of protection of positive energy and power to protect a person from negative energies.

For the person who wears it, they are sure to awaken to a higher degree of consciousness which is sure to help them enhance their intuition.

Amethyst helps in cleaning the aura of a person, and at the same time, it helps a person remain clearheaded even in times of difficulties and confusion. amethyst helps a person remain in control and become the best version of oneself and as a result that is sure to help a person in all sectors of their lives, be it in the family or a job or wherever. It will help you become a person who can make more responsible decisions in life and thus take the best advantage of any given situation.

Apatite

It is not a very known gemstone, but it has significant uses. However, it needs to be kept in mind that they are very brittle in nature and thus have to be handled with care.

It sits on number 5 on the Moh scale of hardness, and apatites can be found in yellow, green, violets, browns, and also blues. And they have a unique and beautiful hexagonal shape. If one has to look for a perfect apatite for themselves, they need to keep in mind that the intenser the color, the better the quality of the stone. So, do not settle for a lighter-colored apatite.

As far as enhancing your psychic abilities are concerned, and the uses of apatite are concerned, they are very helpful in reducing anger levels in a person and also help them keep their stress levels in check.

Apatites help a person enhance their creativity levels and caters to being a positive force behind pumping up a person's imagination. Intuition, which is one of the most important things necessary for enhancing a person's psychic abilities, is something that apatite helps enhance in a person. One can go for apatite bracelets or, for that matter, apatite necklaces or rings.

Keeping this stone near you will help you relax a lot, and your judgments will not get clouded, which will help you get a clear vision of what's happening. The green-colored apatite will also help you to soothe your nervous system while at the same time helping you to maintain your inner balance.

Azurite

Azurite is a very soft gemstone sitting on a 3.5-4 on the Moh scale of hardness. They are usually found alongside malachite and also in places with copper deposits as azurites are byproducts of copper. It is interesting to know that azurites are not only used as gemstones for both jewelry purposes and to enhance psychic abilities, but they are also used as dyes for their beautiful colors as they come in beautiful shades of green and a mixture of blue and green, making a lovely combination.

This gemstone helps a person stimulate their third-eye chakra, which is extremely helpful in enhancing one's psychic abilities.

What happens as a result of that is the inner vision of the concerned person and their dreams get enhanced. Azurite is sure to help a person learn new concepts by making them more receptive to changes and new things. It helps increase a person's insight because the mind becomes calmer, the understanding level of a person gets enhanced.

This helps a person make more productive connections with people, which will invariably open new gates for the person concerned, helping them more opportunities on their way.

Azurite is indeed very helpful for people whose work needs them to take firm decisions based on their intuitions and also for students as they are in the age of grasping new things and concepts and also on the verge of meeting new people and they need to get hold of more and more productive opportunities. It has its own healing purposes and is very famous among spiritual practitioners.

Blue Calcite

This is the gemstone that will help you explore your unconscious in great detail and in deeper intensity.

Blue calcite will help a person to unblock all their creative resources and source of inspiration while at the same time, this stone will help a person to dissolve any limiting believes that they might be having regarding anything. Blue calcite helps a person to strengthen their positive outlook, which invariably acts as a source of power and strength for the concerned person to try and succeed in new things.

Wearing blue calcite will help a person to broaden their horizon of dreaming and exploring life, and a person will become open to changes in life and new possibilities. What is also very interesting to know is that blue calcite helps a person from all sectors of life that does not only do it help a person become emotionally and mentally strong by taking away the extra baggage of worries and anxiety that we tend to carry all the time, it also helps a person remain physically healthy. Blue calcite is a very good choice to get one's psychic abilities enhanced.

If one combines blue calcite with a blue opal or blue chalcedony, it will tend to have an increasing effect on helping a person get rid of the creative blocks from their path. How it does this is by stimulating the third eye vision, which helps in further dismantling the negative beliefs in a person's mind.

Dumortierite

Dumortierite is basically an aluminum boro-silicide mineral and has a beautiful dark blue or indigo color. It is also possible to find this gemstone in other colors such as violet, blue-green or red-brown.

These stones tend to get crystallized and can be found in metamorphic rocks.
This gorgeous, blue in color, gemstone of indigo color is one that greatly enhances a person's psychic and as well as their mental abilities.

Dumortierite helps a person become more insightful and increases a person's understanding abilities. This gemstone helps you gain more insight into any given situation as it will surely help you look at a situation more clearly and with greater practicality.

All your mental and psychic abilities get a channel through which one can guide their spiritual energy. Tarot readers, as well as psychic practitioners, prefer this gemstone as this helps a person give focus on one's self-awareness.

One of the most potent abilities of this stone is to strengthen a person's mental discipline, which helps a person look at things differently with much more patience and with deep understanding.

At times if a person feels emotionally stuck to a certain thing, this gemstone can help take the person out of that situation by helping to find clarity. New pathways are sure to be opened in front of a person who is using this gemstone as divine guidance is sure to come.

One might easily wear this stone in their rings, bracelets, necklaces, or pendants as they are beautiful to look at while at the same time having the above-mentioned uses.

Iolite

Iolite is a beautiful gemstone of violet color and is also known as cordierite, and it is a silicate of magnesium and that of aluminum.

We usually find this stone in places like Madagascar, Sri Lanka, India, Brazil, etc. An Iolite is sure to enhance a person's ability to meditate for a long time with full concentration as it helps a person become calm and composed. It helps a person to remain in more control of their thoughts and subsequent actions as well.

This gemstone helps facilitate a person's inner vision strongly, including a person's shamanic abilities.

Iolite, as a gemstone, helps create a strong bond between the rational mind and the non-rational energies in a person. It is sure to enhance the powers and strengths of a person's inner soul and spiritual core.

It helps a person in reaching the depths of their heart and helps them become more comfortable and confident about their intuitions. If used properly, an Iolite can help a person study their unconscious in detail, thereby creating an understanding in the person of the past and the present.

It will invariably be helpful in resolving issues that had remain pending so far, helping a person to bring forth their innate creativity and potentiality. This gemstone can be easily worn through bracelets, earrings, or necklaces. Pendants, rings, or even raw stones can be used.

Kyanite

Kyanite is a kind of aluminum silicate mineral, and that is the reason it is usually blue in color, but at the same time, they could be found in other colors as well, like white or black, green, grey, orange, and sometimes even pink.

If it is sold in its raw form, it can easily break off into splinters, and that is why it is good to be very careful while you are handling them if you don't know how to or you are not a professional.

One might use this stone in necklaces, in rings, in pendants, or bracelets. Raw kyanite can be kept with oneself, but that is not an easy thing to do.

As mentioned earlier, kyanites have different colors, and they tend to have different properties about themselves. For example, suppose the gemstone is of blue color. In that case, that kyanite helps a person enhance their communication powers and will also help the person transfer energy mind-to-mind, that is, between the conscious mind and the unconscious of the dream world.

It will help the person break away from the chain of complex twisted dreams, making them more lucid and less complicated. This happens as the mind feels less pressure due to the effect of the stone.

The bridge between the physical and the astral body becomes stronger, making the person more in control of himself and his subconscious thoughts. The kyanite will help the concerned person communicate easily with the disparate parts of the self and between the disparate parts of different people.

Labradorite

If one is familiar with the entire practice of tarot card reading, then they will know that this gemstone is a must for any such practice.

Every good tarot reader needs good labradorite for themselves to help them in practice. Labradorite helps a person enhance their multi-layers of awareness of the reality around us, and that is why with shamans, this gem is a must and with those who work with the Akashic records.

This gem helps a person keep their aura very strong and protected as they help to block any intruders. The concerned person will also be helped by being able to remember their experience while they were traveling through the other realms or when they recall their past life memories.

To enhance one's psychic powers, one needs to use their spiritual energies to a great extent. They need to make use of their telepathy skills, their clairvoyance abilities. At the same time, they need to use their divination powers and astral projection while all along maintain communication with their spirit entities.

So, one needs to be emotionally, physically, and mentally strong and confident to go ahead with their practice for all these things. Labradorite helps a person get clarity on all these things and a mastery over them over time.

Lapis Lazuli

Lapis Lazuli is usually blue as it is mainly made up of calcite and lazurite. History tells that this stone was extremely famous in ancient Egypt among the then emperors as it is known to bestow people with wisdom. Beautiful to look at, they are either blue or indigo in color.

The name itself means a deep sense of self-knowledge and self-awareness. This stone has a storehouse of royal energy in it, which invariably helps a person to tap into their core, and that helps a person to uncover and also get access to their innermost noble nature of divine energy and power.

Lapis lazuli is very helpful in activating psychic powers and intuitive abilities. This stone tends to bridge the gap between a person and his spiritual awareness so that it becomes easier to become aware of them and give and receive guidance for the same.

The power that this stone gives helps a person to discern the truth, and at the same time, it helps a person discover their truest selves.

A person can use this gemstone in bracelets, necklaces, pendants, or even earrings. They can also be worn as rings or as a string of beads. Raw Lapis Lazuli can also be kept with oneself.

Magnesite

It is a very soft magnesium carbonate mineral, and that is why it is usually white in color but could also be yellow at times or even brown or grey. It can be mistaken for another gemstone known as turquoise though they are not related at all.

This gemstone can be used in various industrial processes as well. It's a stone that helps balance a person's emotional turmoil by making one receptive to changes and different kinds of situations in life.

It helps a person control what's happening in their lives so that they could be well prepared for any changes that might occur. Magnesite helps enhance a person's higher consciousness whereby they can easily discern their inner core truth and their heart's desires.

This gemstone also helps a person to deeply experience spiritual communication and transcendence as well. The chakra centers are always alert with the help of this stone which further enhances the awakening of the third eye.

This helps the person to get in touch with all the spiritual realms.

A person's psychic awareness is sure to get enhanced as clearer messages will be available to them with the help of this gemstone. Once again, this stone can be used as necklaces, rings, bracelets, pendants, or as earrings. It can as well be kept with a person in its raw form.

Mookaite Jasper

This stone has a very distinct reddish-purple, yellow and brown coloring at times known as mook jasper or the ozokerite. As it is mostly found in Australia, it is at times known as the Australian jasper as well.

It is a rock that is usually formed from sediments that are rich in Silicate, and that is what makes an opaque chalcedony, which is a subclass of quartz. This gemstone is also a form of radiolarite.

As this stone is a vibrant mixture of many colors, as a result of that, it gets connected to our root chakra (red and brown mookaite), to our solar plexus (yellow mookaite), and our third eye (purple mookaite). That is the reason psychics find it very interesting to work with this stone, as it always garners a unique response.

This helps a person to remain young at heart as it helps change our perspectives towards things, and also it helps shape our mentality in a positive direction. Mookaite helps us connect our inner spiritual strength with that of the earth and aligns our spiritual energy with that of our ancestors who have walked this earth before us.

This has an intense effect on our emotional terrain, helping us understand and transform our emotional patterns and behaviors in a way that has been passed down to us by our ancestors. This understanding has great healing powers and is extremely beneficial for a person.

Moonstone

It is a feldspar mineral gemstone, and it is pale and iridescent. It looks really similar to some opals, but they are chemically very different.

Moonstone is usually milky-white, and the iridescence is usually gray, blue, or peach in tone. One might use this stone in bracelets, or rings, or necklaces and earrings. White moonstone jewelry is very popular as they are beautiful to look at. Raw moonstone could also be carried with oneself.

Moonstone is filled with a sort of feminine power and mystery, and it helps a person enhance their journey inwards by finding looking for and finding truths that might be hidden in our unconscious and also in our past lives.

Intuition, which is one of the primary necessities of a psychic, gets enhanced by a moonstone, and it also encourages our level of patience and trust in our divine timing. If one is familiar with the practice of tarot reading, then it is a known fact that the priestess card has to always correspond with the moonstone.

Moonstone helps a person stimulate the brain's thinking process, which allows the concerned person to take confident leaps in their insight without having to wait for a long time. So, a moonstone is a must if a person wants to connect themselves with their femininity, be it whether male or female.

Pietersite

This gemstone is a form of quartz that comes in a host of different shades like mottled brown, blue, gold, and grey. It contains the tiger eye, which gives it the chatoyancy effect. However, this gemstone is only found in China and Namibia. It could be worn in bracelets, necklaces, pendants, rings, earrings, as well as raw stones, can be carried.

This stone is extremely helpful for people who feel that they are stuck in the world of their inner thoughts and feel a bit shook up with the problems they are facing.

This gemstone helps people calm down their anxieties and get a sense of purpose to decide the correct direction for themselves. If at any point you feel blocked, or lost, or uncertain, this stone is sure to help you out of it as it will help you get your spiritual core get aligned with your intentions and desires.

Pietersite can help you bring a kind of spiritual catharsis in a person as it will help clear all the stagnant energies and help you recognize your true intentions. This stone helps build a connection between the third chakra and the sixth chakra, which enhances a person's willpower and intuition.

Conclusion

Thank you for making it through to the end of *Empath and Psychic Abilities*, let's hope it was informative and able to provide you with all of the tools you need to achieve your goals, whatever they may be.

If you found this book useful in any way, a review on Amazon is always appreciated!

www.ingramcontent.com/pod-product-compliance
Ingram Content Group UK Ltd.
Pitfield, Milton Keynes, MK11 3LW, UK
UKHW020138250726
13967UKWH00002B/740

9 780645 081565